365

STYLE AND FASHION TIPS FOR MEN

Claudia Piras and
Bernhard Roetzel

D1363717

DUMONT
monte

The authors:
Claudia Piras is an author and freelance journalist writing for various lifestyle magazines. In addition to her interest in culinary matters, she also specializes in the fields of fashion and living trends. Bernhard Roetzel is a freelance fashion journalist and contributes regularly to established magazines such as "Men's Health" and "Manager Magazine," as well as numerous other fashiontrade publications. He has already published several books on fashion.

Cover illustrations: Montblanc Deutschland GmbH, Hamburg (www.montblanc.com), d'Avenza fashion S.p.A., Avenza (www.davenza.com), Crockett & Jones Ltd., Northampton (www.crocketandjones.co.uk)

Original edition
© 2002 DuMont monte Verlag, Cologne
All rights reserved.

Author: Claudia Piras and Bernhard Roetzel
Production: Königsblau, Nicole Gehlen
Translation: Susan Ghanouni in association with First Edition Translations Ltd
Editing: David Price in association with First Edition Translations Ltd
Typesetting: First Edition Translations Ltd, Cambridge, UK
Overall production: Mladinska, Slowenien

ISBN 3-8320-7123-7
Printed in Slovenia

Contents

BASIC BUSINESS WEAR:
SUIT, SHIRT, AND TIE

Some men regard a suit as a necessary evil that must be worn from Monday to Friday, while others love every minute of wearing their fine business garb. Regardless of whether you are a reluctant or willing follower of your company's dress code, however, an immaculate appearance will at least give you a sense of inner calm and confidence.

1

In continental Europe, the standard outfit for business functions and special occasions is a dark gray, single-breasted suit. In Britain, however, navy blue tends to be the preferred color for suits. Gray flannel, herringbone, and Prince of Wales check are popular in America.

The more often you need to wear a suit, the greater number of suits you will need. This will also enable you to experiment with some of the more unusual colors. If you only possess a small number of suits, however, restrict yourself to the undisputed classic colors and patterns.

Pinstripes and chalkstripes are regarded as the accepted uniform of the business world. They are the favorite style worn by London bankers and stockbrokers. The story goes that this preference originates in the fact that the stripes resemble the lines on an account sheet.

3

4

If you are planning to iron a suit, jacket, or pair of trousers, do not use a hot iron directly on the fabric. Always place a clean cotton or linen cloth over the garment you are ironing to prevent the material becoming shiny.

5

Treat your suit jackets, blazers, sports jackets, and coats to good coat hangers with broad, rounded shoulder supports. This will help your clothes keep their shape however long they are left on hangers.

A good sense of style means wearing suits appropriate to the different seasons. This does not necessarily imply that only thick, heavy materials should be worn in winter. A lightweight worsted flannel is equally suitable for the colder months.

7

If you always wear a suit to the office, you should invest in a classic woolen winter coat. Dark gray and dark blue are the most formal colors, while beige or camel is better suited to more casual wear.

8

Black is not a suitable color for a business suit except as a background color to white pinstripes.

9

The most classic style of suit is the single-breasted type with three buttons and side vents, with the double-breasted suit coming a close second. The single-breasted suit with two buttons, however, is more often out of fashion than in. The same is true of the single-button version.

If you have a large, prominent backside, a central vent at the back of your jacket will serve to emphasize this feature. Men of this build should stick to jackets with side vents or no vents at all.

10

11

You should always keep your jacket on during a business meeting with a client, as you will not look very professional in shirt sleeves. If you find this too warm, wear a more lightweight material.

12 Only entrust your suits to a reliable dry-cleaning establishment as this is the only place you will get them professionally pressed.

13 Suits with a vest should ideally be made from a lighter material otherwise you will soon be perspiring in this combination.

14

Light-gray suits are unsuitable for evening occasions, as darker shades are *de rigueur* once the sun has set. Whether you choose charcoal gray or navy is up to you.

15

If you want to adopt an elegant Italian look, stipulate that your autumn and winter suits should be left unlined or semi-lined when you order them. No one else will notice any difference, but you will enjoy the advantage of never feeling too warm indoors.

If you need to wear a suit at the office from Monday to Friday, you should have at least two in your wardrobe. This allows each one a day's rest after being worn.

16

17

Cotton or linen suits are popular summer classics. The problem is that they can very quickly come to resemble Columbo's raincoat. Extra lightweight wool, on the other hand, does not crease quite so easily.

If you want to score a few style points in Italy in spring or autumn, wear an unlined Solaro suit. This is an English fabric which shimmers red, blue, or green on the underside.

18

19

Your shirt collar must stick up at least a quarter inch above your jacket. Otherwise, when you sit down, you might find your shirt disappearing beneath the collar of your jacket.

20

Most men buy shirts with collars that are too wide for them and sleeves that are too short. Your collar is the correct size if it is a snug fit and does not bunch up under your tie. Your sleeves are the correct length if you have about a quarter inch of cuff protruding from the sleeve of your jacket.

21

White is the classic color for business shirts. Since white does not suit everyone, however, light blue may be worn as an alternative and is compatible with most complexions.

22

On a button-down shirt, the collar points do not necessarily have to be fastened. If left open, they create a more Italian-style casual look.

23

Avoid short-sleeved shirts for the office. These should be kept strictly for leisure wear, unless the atmosphere in your office is very casual, in which case you should dispense with a tie as well.

24

Roll your sleeves down before donning your jacket otherwise you will look as if you are wearing a short-sleeved shirt.

25

For a television appearance, you would do well to choose a light blue shirt as this is the most flattering color to wear on screen.

26

Anyone with a good eye for quality will look first at a shirt's side seam. The narrowness of the seam speaks for the quality of the garment. This detail only becomes apparent, however, when you unpack the shirt from its wrapping.

27

In the case of made-to-measure shirts, the width of the cuffs varies to allow room for a watch, depending on whether you wear it on your left or right wrist.

28

You can double the life of your shirt if you have its worn-out collar or cuffs replaced. Either a section of the original material can be borrowed from the shirt-tail for this purpose, or else a new piece of white material can be used.

29

Shirts should not be placed in the tumbler after washing as they can easily shrink in high temperatures.

30

On no account should a T-shirt be visible under the open neck of a business shirt. No one wants to see your underwear.

31

A shirt is easier to iron if it is still slightly damp.

32

A monogram is more discreet if it is placed on the left shirt front on a level with the navel. It is too conspicuous on a cuff or breast pocket.

33

Hand-embroidered monograms are usually done in capital letters. You can recognize machine-stitched ones by the fact that they are usually done in script form.

34

A custom suit should not only be tailored to fit the body, but also to fit your personality. So a good tailor needs to be a good judge of character.

English etiquette regards it as a sign of good breeding and understatement to have one's sleeve buttons done up correctly. In Italy, however, it is quite acceptable to leave the lower button undone as a subtle means of drawing attention to the quality of your suit.

35

36

Made-to-measure mass-produced garments constitute a standard menu, in which the variable factor is the main course. In the case of genuine tailor-made articles, on the other hand, you yourself are in a position to choose the starter, the main course, and the dessert, according to your personal preferences.

The term "made-to-measure" does not always mean genuine garments that are custom-made. A professional tailor will design a pattern exclusively for you, whereas tailored factory-made garments are cut to a standard size and then altered to fit your measurements.

37

Should you decide to have a suit made by a tailor, be guided by personal recommendation. Just trusting to luck in your choice of tailor would be very foolish as standards of quality can vary considerably.

38

39

The best kind of shirt buttons are made from mother-of-pearl, this being a more attractive alternative to plastic, as well as being harder and tougher.

The fabric of a summer shirt should be lightweight and have an open weave. This will ensure that fresh air can circulate and obviate the need for an unattractive short-sleeved style.

41

In hot weather, avoid wearing shirts with double cuffs as they can make your wrists unnecessarily warm. In the casual style of the Italians, at least, it is also perfectly acceptable to leave single cuffs unbuttoned under your jacket.

42

Because of its thick interlining, a stiff shirt collar is likely to make you perspire heavily in summer. A button-down type of shirt is pleasanter to wear, as the collar is not reinforced.

43

Before you wear your new shirt for the first time, it should be washed at least once. This will rinse out any residual manufacturing chemicals and make the material softer.

44

If your shirts are of good quality, the buttons will not come off after a couple of weeks, as they will have been sewn on by hand. Alternatively, you can reinforce the machine-sewn buttons, making sure you tie off the thread with a firm knot.

45 The simplest way to test the quality of a necktie is to hold it at its narrow end and let it hang down. If it looks twisted, it is an indication that the silk has not been cut at the correct 45-degree angle.

46 Never toss your necktie back over your shoulder to stop it dangling in your soup. Nor should you tuck it down your shirt. The answer is to take a bit more care when you are eating.

Neckties made from silk, cashmere, or wool, should never be washed. This does not, of course, apply to synthetic ties, but you really should not admit to having such a thing.

47

48

An elegantly dressed man will either tie his necktie in a simple slip knot or wear it in an Albert knot, a large knot made by making extra turns when tying the tie. He will avoid Windsor knots (half or whole) altogether, as the triangular form does not fit snugly into the collar.

It is not as difficult as you might think to tie a bow tie. Try it out first by tying it as if you were tying up a shoe-lace, but practicing around your thigh. After a few times, it will have become second nature to you and you will be able to repeat the procedure just as easily around your neck.

50

Never try to smooth out crumpled neckties by ironing them. All you need to do is roll up your tie and the creases will come out by themselves.

The best way to remove really stubborn creases in neckties is by giving them a steam bath. You can use either the steam from your iron or a saucepan of boiling water for this purpose.

51

52

Knitted cotton neckties are a cooler alternative to silk ones in the summer months.

53

Under no circumstances should you resort to a ready-knotted necktie. If you are unable to tie your own tie, it is high time you learnt to do so. If you are in no mind to do so, the best advice is to forget about wearing a tie altogether.

Never be tempted to leave your necktie knotted in order to avoid having to re-knot it. At the end of a long day, first loosen the knot carefully, then lift it over your head, before finally undoing the knot properly.

54

Anyone with a keen fashion sense will have at least as many cashmere ties as silk ones, providing a stylish autumn alternative that can be worn with a sports jacket as well as with a dark business suit.

55

56

If you know someone who is very fond of neckties and you want to give him something special, buy him a sevenfold tie. This consists of material that has been folded seven times into layers, its very volume making a lining unnecessary.

If wearing a necktie feels like sheer torture between May and August, it is not only due to the silk. The cotton lining will make it feel even hotter.

57

58

Loosely woven neckties, preferably unlined, are ideal for summer. Lightweight knitted silk or cotton ties are also recommended for this time of year. The more open the weave, the more air they will allow through.

59

Is the point of your necktie irresistibly drawn towards bowls of soup? The best solution is to wear a bow tie. With the best will in the world, you will not be able to dip this in the soup.

60

Be wary of brown neckties. In London, this color is regarded as being completely unsuitable for business.

A black or dark-gray necktie is obligatory for a funeral. If you opt instead for a silk bow tie, ensure it is not a very shiny one. Black knitted silk is a very elegant alternative to wear for a funeral.

61

62

As a rule of thumb, wool neckties are too casual for a dark business suit. A silk tie is what you should wear to the office.

QUALITY IN LEATHER:
SHOES

Your shoes are – in the truest sense of the word – the basis on which your overall appearance rests. If these do not go with the rest of your outfit, then all your efforts with your suit, shirt, and tie will virtually count for nothing. Not only should shoes for business and evening be chosen with care, but casual shoes deserve similar careful consideration. Leisure time, after all, accounts for a large part of our lives.

63

The rear third of the shoe, in other words, the instep and heel, must be a perfect fit. If it is too wide across this part, the rest of your foot will press too far forward into the toe of the shoe.

The most conservative type of shoe
is the stout, black Oxford. The brogue,
with its pattern of tiny holes, is
regarded as somewhat sportier.

64

"No brown after six" used to be the rule in England. This used to apply not just to footwear, but to your entire outfit. Gentlemen would change for dinner into black evening dress, so brown shoes were consequently completely out of the question.

65

66

Never wear the same pair of shoes two days in a row. You should always leave your shoes to rest for at least 24 hours after each wearing.

67

Unless you want to stew your feet in their own juices during the summer months, you would be well advised to leave your heavy leather shoes with their double soles at home in the wardrobe. Lightweight, linen-lined Oxfords would be a much more suitable alternative.

If the weather is hot, loafers or slip-on shoes allow more air to circulate round your feet than lace-ups or buckled shoes, which can also impair circulation in your feet and legs.

68

69

Regardless of whether or not fashion or summery temperatures suggest otherwise, sandals have been "out" since the fall of the Roman Empire.

70

In English financial circles, loafers are regarded as too casual for business wear. Black lace-ups are a more appropriate choice. Classic Oxford shoes, or half brogues with a discreet pattern of tiny holes, are the best choice to aim for.

71

Never wear red shoes, unless you happen to be the Pope.

Loafers should be quite a tight fit across the instep when you first get them. They will then fit properly once you have worn them in. If they are loose to start with, they will become too wide later on.

72

73

Never wear Jesus-style open sandals, unless you are the Messiah. If fresh air is so essential to your feet, then it would be better to go without shoes altogether.

74

Sports shoes are not a suitable footwear to wear with a suit. Keep shoes of this kind for your free time or for running in. The only exception to this are top-of-the-range running shoes, so-called designer sneakers.

75

Brogues and shoes with stitched seams are less suitable for formal occasions than simple Oxfords or similar types of shoe.

If you are wearing shoes with a buckled strap, the color of the metal buckle must match that of your belt. Brass goes with brass and gold, silver goes with silver.

77

There is no need to compromise with made-to-measure shoes. The Duke of Windsor once complained when the Parisian shoemaker Berluti punched three holes in the straps of a pair of buckled shoes. The latter accepted the complaint when his royal client pointed out quite rightly that "with a pair of made-to-measure shoes, the strap should only need one hole, namely in the exact spot it is needed."

Well-polished, reasonably priced shoes make a better impression than uncared-for luxury ones. Taking care of your shoes in this way is not just important for their outward appearance, but also helps to prolong their life.

78

79

Having the necessary repairs carried out to your shoes prolongs their life. Make sure you have a new rubber heel fitted before the leather gets damaged, and have them resoled before the inner sole is affected.

Never have a rubber sole put onto the
leather sole of a welted shoe as
this will spoil the balance of the whole shoe.

80

Shoes with synthetic soles are the best footwear for rainy days (you can get these with welted soles too). If you don't feel these are elegant enough to wear with your business suit, protect your leather soles in wet weather by wearing rubber galoshes.

81

You should wear dark knee-length socks with your business suit and lighter-colored ones with casualwear. In your free time, however, you can dispense with socks altogether – weather permitting.

83

You can darken the color of your light-colored leather shoes with dark wax polish, but be careful: it is very difficult to reverse the process if too much color is applied. It is best to build up the color very gradually from light to dark.

84

Is it OK to dispense with knee-length socks in hot weather? Unfortunately not. A hairy shin above short socks is not a pretty sight even in summer.

Any shoes with artificial soles should be kept for
leisure wear. Leather is by far the more elegant choice
for business.

If you have new shoes with leather soles, wear them a couple of times in dry weather before venturing out in the rain in them. This will make the leather more water-resistant.

86

87

Always use a shoehorn when putting your shoes on. This protects the top edge of the heel. Forcing your heel into your shoe will also pull your socks down or wrinkle them.

Always put a shoe tree inside your shoes after each wearing. It will help keep your footwear in shape for years, if not decades. Even cheap, simple types of shoe tree, available from any department store, are perfectly adequate. Expensive versions that have to be screwed into position are best left for the specialist.

88

89

If leather soles have become damp, lay the shoes on their side (with a shoe tree inserted). Similarly, if your feet tend to sweat heavily, it is best to store your shoes on their side.

90

Never put wet shoes to dry on a radiator or next to a direct source of heat, as this will cause the leather to become brittle and cracked.

91

For best results when cleaning your shoes, rub on some shoe polish in the evening and leave overnight. In this way, the polish will have had chance to work its way into the leather and the shoes will be much easier to polish.

92

Wax shoe polish is much easier to apply if it is warmed a little before use. Stand the can in the sun for a short while in summer, or on a radiator in winter.

93

When cleaning your shoes, do not forget the edges around the sole, or the outside and inside of the heel. A small amount of polish here will help prevent moisture getting in.

94

Do not overstretch the shoe with an overextended shoe tree. As a rule of thumb, lace-ups require less pressure than loafers.

95

Wear laboratory or household gloves when cleaning your shoes, as this will protect your hands from stubborn stains. Wear an apron or overall to protect your clothes.

96

The most efficient way to polish your shoes is with a large horsehair brush. You can then buff them to a lovely shine afterwards using a soft polishing cloth. Alternatively, you can use the sort of soft cloth which some makes of shoe include in the shoe box.

When applying the polish with a brush, you are bound to get tiny drops of shoe cream spattering in all directions. That is why it is a good idea to wear an apron or overalls, or shine the shoes using a rolled up pair of ladies' pantyhose.

97

98

If polishing shoes is not your favorite pastime, you would be well advised to buy suede shoes. The only care these require is regular brushing and an application of shoe polish to the edges of the leather soles.

If you do not have a shoe horn handy, slip your heel into the shoe by sliding it down a handkerchief. Do make sure, of course, that you unlace your shoe completely before trying to put it on.

99   100

Never wear cowboy boots with a suit or with a jacket and trousers. They are only suitable with jeans. You should also avoid unauthentic boots with heels that are too flat, too angled, or legs that are too short.

101

Be wary about wearing shoes with higher heels, like ankle boots, for example, particularly with formal suits.

Do not wear winter boots lined with lambs' wool with a business outfit. If your feet get cold in lightweight lace-ups, wear your warm footwear on your way to and from work and slip your proper shoes on when you get to the office.

102

103

Do not tie your laces up too tightly on a long flight, as this could impair the circulation in your legs.

SMART CASUAL

A pullover thrown loosely around the shoulders, elegant sports shoes or loafers, sunglasses pushed up on top of the head – we are all familiar with the chic Italian casual look from holidays or from films. People born in Italy, however, do not automatically have the monopoly on casual elegance. Anyone can achieve it by mastering the basic rules of the smart-casual look.

104

An outfit is considered smart casual if casual clothes are teamed with individual smart items, for example, by wearing a silver-buckled leather belt with faded jeans, a cashmere pullover over a polo shirt, espadrilles with a white summer suit.

105

Short trousers are fine for leisure wear, as long as the occasion does not warrant more formal dress – provided that you have reasonable-looking legs. Do not wear knee-length socks, though – it is better to wear your shoes without any socks at all.

If you are dressing all in denim, then choose a shirt, pair of trousers, and jacket either in exactly the same shade, or else in contrasting colors. A random combination of denim clothes rarely looks stylish.

106

107

A round- or V-necked sweater is something you can wear all year round. In summer, you can sling it around your shoulders or around your hips, while in cold weather, you can wear it around your neck (in place of a scarf). Or you could just put it on and wear it properly!

108

The clothes you wear for the office should play no part in your casual wardrobe. Avoid anything that is part of your business outfit, such as black lace-up shoes, gray jackets, or coats.

Why not experiment with new fashion trends as part of your leisure wardrobe? Swap your chinos for a pair of cargo pants (baggy trousers with pockets at thigh level), or wear a hooded top instead of a pullover and a padded vest instead of your quilted jacket.

109

110

The appropriate headgear with the smart casual look is a baseball cap in summer and a woolen hat in winter. If possible, go without a hat altogether, since going hatless is by far the best option.

111

Never press a crease into your jeans. This would conflict with the casual character of your denim jeans.

The most popular type of leisure wear pants are chinos. Worn with a polo shirt, they look very casual, but teaming them with a blue jacket would elevate the look to smart casual. A word of warning: chinos should not be too creased or baggy. So, give them a quick iron before wearing (flat, no center crease).

If you like to adopt a casual look, yet still want to appear well-groomed, your best option is to wear an ironed polo shirt. A good choice for winter is the long-sleeved version.

114

113

Never wear black or gray cotton chinos. The reason for this is that these types of pants were originally part of the US uniform in the Pacific. The correct colors are therefore military ones, such as white, beige, khaki, or olive green.

115

Within continental Europe, a navy blue blazer with gold buttons is often worn as a business outfit. However, in America, as in England, the home of the blazer, it would be classed more as a smart casual look.

116

If polo shirts are your favorite type of leisure wear, why not try a long-sleeved version when the weather gets cold. The short-sleeved summer style looks rather out of place between the months of October and May.

A good-quality padded jacket, quilted vest, or parka is a good investment since it can be worn both for the office as well as in your free time. You may find yourself out on a limb fashionwise, however, as your conservative colleagues may well look down their noses at your choice of a Woolrich parka over pinstripes.

118 117

If you do not like wearing a necktie at the weekend, but the occasion demands something a little bit formal, wear a rollneck sweater with your suit, or a fine merino wool polo shirt.

119

Your waxed jacket is still an indispensable autumn classic and can just as easily be worn with jeans, a sweater, and canvas shoes, as with a business suit.

120

A navy blue jacket is perfect for all leisure-time occasions. Worn with jeans, this jacket looks casual, whereas teamed with gray wool trousers, it looks smart enough for a sophisticated restaurant.

If you get too warm in woolen sweaters, try a sweatshirt instead, or a light quilted vest over a polo shirt. Alternatively, opt for one of the zippered knitted jackets that are currently in fashion again.

121

Sleeveless pullovers are very practical for wearing under a jacket. However, the advantage of one with sleeves is that it can be thrown casually round your shoulders or tied round your hips.

122

123

If you are not quite sure about the dress code for a forthcoming weekend invitation, then the safest thing to pack is a corduroy jacket. If the atmosphere is casual, then substitute the trousers with a pair of chinos or jeans. A more formal look can be achieved by wearing a necktie.

124

If you are wearing white jeans, team them with a contrasting color of shirt, pullover, or jacket. It is not a good idea to wear an all-white outfit for casualwear.

125

Black jeans were very popular in the 1980s. Today, classic blue is back in fashion again because its appearance improves the more it is washed, whereas black denim eventually turns an unattractive gray after repeated washings.

126

A sports jacket goes equally well with flannel trousers as with a pair of jeans. If you decide on denim, dispense with the necktie.

127

Leather jackets are ideal for leisure wear. Shades of brown and bright colors create a more casual look, whereas black can be very severe.

128

Never wear a necktie with a leather blouson jacket. A tie is only ever worn with a suit or sports-type jacket. The only people who wear ties with leather jackets are the sidekicks of detective inspectors in 1970s TV serials.

129

No matter how comfortable you feel in them, never appear outside your own four walls in tracksuit pants unless you are going jogging.

130

Never wear tracksuit pants around the house, unless you are alone. This is not a sight you should inflict on others.

131

Having cotton trousers dry-cleaned, instead of washing them in the washing machine, helps them keep their shape.

You cannot go wrong wearing brown or beige corduroy pants with a tweed jacket. Unfortunately, these colors often seem a little boring. Experiment with pink, moss green, burgundy, sky blue, or rust red for a change!

132

TUXEDOS AND EVENING DRESS

If you want to look your best for an extra special occasion, you will have to pull out all the stops and wear a tuxedo, tails, or cutaway. But the mere thought of such a formal event is enough to make some people break out in a cold sweat. It should, in fact, be something you can look forward to, and once you are familiar with the basic rules governing such an occasion, you will be able to do just that.

133

The correct attire for special daytime occasions is morning dress. Because of its long tails, the jacket is also known as a "daytime tailcoat." Historically speaking, this term is not quite accurate as it evolved in actual fact from the frock coat.

134

Morning dress comprises a black or dark gray tailcoat, a light-colored, usually gray or buff vest, and gray and black striped trousers.

135

The only appropriate headgear to wear with morning dress is a top hat.

136

A somewhat less formal alternative to morning dress is achieved if you replace the tailcoat with a black jacket. This style was popular all over Europe at the beginning of the 20th century.

137

If you are attending an outdoor function or one on board ship, you can exchange your black tuxedo for a light-colored dinner jacket.

If you are wearing morning or evening dress, position the tails to the left and right of the chair when you sit down. This will avoid unsightly creases.

138

139

A cummerbund, i.e. a broad silk pleated waistband, may be worn with a tuxedo, but never with a tailcoat.

140

Always carry a fresh cotton handkerchief with you, in addition to your own personal one, so that you can offer it to a lady should she need it. If she uses it to have a good "blow," rather than just mopping her brow with it, there is no need to ask for it back.

141

A flat, neat wristwatch with a black leather strap goes better with a tuxedo than a sporty style of watch.

A black evening coat should be worn over your evening dress or tuxedo, with an optional white silk scarf. This must be removed when you arrive, however, unless you want to look like an opera singer.

142

143

Only a white bow tie should be worn with tails, or you might be mistaken for one of the service staff (waiters wear a black bow tie with their evening dress).

144

A black bow tie may be worn with a tuxedo. You can always add a dash of color by tucking a conspicuous silk handkerchief into your breast pocket.

145

Black patent leather shoes are the correct footwear to wear with evening dress. Traditionalists prefer the pump, a flat-heeled, low-cut shoe, adorned with silk ribbon.

146

If you count yourself as one of the elite, your pumps will have the silk-like sheen of calf's leather, as the shine of patent leather is considered somewhat vulgar.

147

Some shoe experts recommend polishing your evening shoes (if made from calf leather, not patent leather) with champagne. This might seem a waste, but the carbonic acid does actually intensify the leather's shine. However, you can achieve the same effect using cheap sparkling wine.

148

If you are likely to wear morning dress more than once a year, perhaps you should consider the possibility of buying an outfit (rather than hiring one). A dark gray one is the most versatile, in other words, a jacket, vest, and trousers that are all in charcoal gray.

149

An effective way of adding a touch of eccentricity to your tuxedo is to wear unusual socks. Deep violet socks, for example, would be both eye-catching and stylish.

The trousers of your evening dress or cutaway should be held up by suspenders (or braces as they are called in England), as opposed to a belt. This enables the vest to lie flush against the trouser waistband. If you really cannot abide suspenders, then make sure your trousers have an adjustable waistband with built-in elastic to hold them in place.

150

Striped trousers are the usual companion to a morning coat, but this is not obligatory. Pillars of fashion may prefer light-gray trousers in a time houndstooth check in summer, and glen-plaid cloth is another interesting alternative. If your surname begins with "Mac" or "Mc", you may prefer to wear Scottish tartan with your black tailcoat.

151

152

In English country houses, a burgundy, blue, or bottle-green velvet smoking jacket is an acceptable alternative to a black tuxedo.

153

You can buy velvet evening shoes to match your smoking jacket. However, if you are a guest at an English country house, only wear such things if you want to signal that you are having an affair with the hostess.

154

Never wear brown with a cutaway, evening dress, or tuxedo.

155

Do not wear a top hat with a dark evening coat over the tuxedo. If you must wear a hat, then make sure it is a derby. Since the traditional derby is hopelessly outdated, however, the best bet is to go without a hat altogether.

For a church wedding, the light gray morning coat is reserved for the bridegroom and his best man. The rest of the male guests should wear black or dark gray.

156

157

On no account let anyone talk you into wearing evening dress with a spencer jacket. This should be worn exclusively by English naval officers as part of their dress uniform.

158

There should be no frills or ruches on your dress shirt, unless you are a pop singer or work as a croupier in Las Vegas.

159

The classic shoes to wear with morning dress are black Oxfords without any decorative perforation, although buckled shoes or slip-on shoes are also permissible, as long as they are made of black leather.

160

At a civil wedding, the bridegroom should wear a dark suit. Morning dress is a more formal alternative for a church ceremony.

Never wear your ordinary everyday shoes with evening dress or a tuxedo. Even if they are made of black leather, they are no substitute for black patent Oxfords or pumps.

161

162

You should never wear a bow tie or patent shoes with morning dress. A long tie and normal calf's leather shoes are the correct accessories for this outfit.

163

A tuxedo is not normally a suitable garment for a wedding, as this is primarily an evening outfit. But for some weddings in the USA, however, you may wear evening black even during the daytime.

164

Black tails are really only intended as evening wear. Very occasionally, you may see them worn by the bridegroom at a very official, aristocratic wedding.

If the dress code calls for tails, you may also wear any decorations or medals you may have. Soldiers may also wear full uniform for such occasions.

165

166

If you are invited to a wedding, let the bridal couple set the tone when it comes to fashion. As a guest, your clothes should never outshine those of the two main characters.

What goes with what?
Mixing and matching

Men usually seem to know it all, have something to say on every subject, and always seem to have an answer for everything. When it comes to choosing the right tie to go with a particular shirt, however, they suddenly find themselves at a loss. Mixing and matching colors, patterns and fabrics is quite obviously not their strong point, even though this is not as difficult as many might think.

167

Every color should be repeated, but only once. Burgundy socks go with a burgundy necktie, for example, but not if your jacket is lined in the same color.

168

It is a popular mistake to assume that a patterned necktie cannot be worn with a patterned shirt. Just remember the following important rule: A tie with small pattern can be worn with a large-patterned shirt, and vice versa.

169

Your necktie and pocket handkerchief should never be the same color (and definitely not made of the same material). Do not be tempted by any tie and handkerchief sets on sale in the stores.

170

Avoid wearing navy-blue socks with black shoes. Black or gray ones are more suitable. Brown socks would be completely out of place, whereas subtle reddish tones would be regarded as acceptable.

171

Never be tempted to use a ready-folded dress handkerchief, or one with just a triangular point. It would be better to do without one at all.

172

There are really only two classic colors for men's shoes, namely brown and black. Green is only suitable for rubber boots.

173

Brown shoes go better with a navy blue suit than black, although the business dress code in English-speaking countries frowns upon this combination.

174

Assemble your outfit in a different order to the one you dress in, working from outside to inside: first the suit, then the shirt, and finally, the tie. Generally speaking, your choice of larger garments will be more limited, so this will have to determine the basic direction of your outfit.

175

White linen is the simplest choice for a pocket handkerchief as it goes with any business suit. Either fold it into a square, or push it loosely into your breast pocket.

If you like silk handkerchiefs, choose a pattern that picks out one of the colors in your necktie. For example, a dark blue tie with red stripes would look good with a dark red paisley handkerchief or a blue silk one with tiny white dots.

176

177

If you are wearing a tweed suit with a woolen necktie, a cashmere handkerchief would be a better alternative to a shiny silk one.

When you are planning your outfit, it is not just the colors you must bear in mind, but the visual effect and feel of the individual garments. Gray wool flannel trousers should not be teamed with highly polished leather shoes, for example, as the contrast would be too stark. Suede leather shoes would be more compatible with flannel material.

179

When mixing and matching colors, ask yourself first if they tone with each other and if they make an interesting combination.

180

The classic colors for business wear are dark-gray or blue tones. Brown and green shades are regarded as being more suitable for casual occasions. This basic fact remains unassailable, no matter how much designers would prefer men to have a freer hand in choosing what colors they wear.

181

If you have a rather reddish complexion, you will find a pale-blue shirt more flattering than a white one, as the latter would merely accentuate any high color. Look out for this next time you are at a business lunch: The face of anyone wearing a white cotton shirt will glow redder with every glass of wine.

182

Be very wary about wearing yellow for business. Never wear a yellow jacket or suit; even a yellow shirt is somewhat questionable. It is a color that is best restricted to a necktie or a pocket handkerchief.

183

If your hair is gray, wear a suit and shirt in a color that contrasts with your silver locks. Light gray does not provide enough of a contrast.

If you have a shock of white hair, this color should be echoed in your clothes, for example in a pinstripe or appropriate shirt. A white suit, however, would be too much of a good thing, the light color becoming too dominant.

184

185

Beige summer suits tend to make central and northern Europeans look pale and washed out. They look much better on men with black hair and dark complexions.

186

Blond-haired and pale-skinned central European types look best in navy blue, light-brown, or medium-gray summer suits.

Summery pastel shades, such as pink, mint green, salmon, or sky blue, should be framed by strong colors, for example a navy-blue jacket.

187

188

Never wear a bright red shirt for business. A bright red necktie, however, is okay, making a very sharp contrast if worn with a white shirt. A light blue cotton shirt, on the other hand, will soften the effect somewhat.

189

As we all know, white tennis socks are an absolute no-no with a dark suit. With a white summer suit and light-colored suede shoes, however, white knee socks are perfectly correct.

A pair of soft flannel or light worsted trousers can be teamed with any color or style of jacket and should be an indispensable part of your wardrobe.

190

191

Avoid wearing a suit, shirt, and necktie all with the same pattern, for example, a glen plaid suit, with a glen plaid shirt and matching tie. The same applies to houndstooth check, herringbone, and shepherd's check.

A plain nondescript gray
is only suitable for suits, pants,
and coats and not for shirts,
ties, or shoes.

192

193

A self-colored or striped shirt goes best with a checked suit. If you are determined to wear a checked shirt with your checked suit, then make sure that the checks are a different size.

194

If you are looking for a necktie to go with a particular suit, you have two options: Either match the color of the silk tie to the basic color of the suit material, or else pick out a particular color from the fabric pattern. With a gray glen plaid with a light blue over-check, you could, for example, wear a dark blue tie with light blue spots.

The classic pinstripe is white on a blue or gray background. Fabrics with colored stripes are rather more unusual. Decide on a pattern that goes with your favorite shirt color: white pinstripes with white cotton, or blue pinstripes with blue cotton.

196 195

The patterns of your necktie, shirt, and suit should be in contrast to one another. A suit with vertical stripes, for example, could be worn with a checked shirt and a diagonally striped tie.

197

When assembling your outfit, try to ensure that the look and feel of your shirt and suit blend well together. A tweed jacket will look best with a plain or twill weave shirt, whereas an extra fine batiste shirt would complement a lightweight worsted material.

198

Never wear a mint-green, lilac, dark-purple, petrol-colored, or ochre-yellow suit for business. The only acceptable colors are dark gray and blue.

199

The more colors contained in your suit fabric, the more difficult it becomes to choose a shirt and necktie to go with it. If you do not have an eye for fashion, it is better to choose a plain fabric.

200

Be careful about wearing colored or patterned socks. Dark self-colored ones are easier to team with the rest of your outfit. Patterned socks do have the advantage, however, of being easier to sort after washing.

201

If you really are hopeless at deciding which colors go well together, stick to gray suits and light-blue shirts. Any tie will look fine with this combination.

202

Be wary of wearing a green suit – you might be mistaken for a forester.

THOSE ALL-IMPORTANT ACCESSORIES

Little things can often produce a remarkably big effect. This is particularly true in the case of fashion accessories. What is a bit of ear piercing, after all, other than a few grams of metal? But it would be guaranteed to hit the world press if the President of the United States were to have his nose pierced. It follows, therefore, that little things like this deserve to be chosen with the utmost care.

203

Visible jewelry should be restricted to two rings (a wedding ring and a dress ring), a watch, and a pair of cuff links. What you wear out of sight under your shirt in the way of chains, lucky charms, bracelets, etc. is your own private business.

Bracelets on men are okay in theory, but still might cause a few raised eyebrows in some conservative circles.

204

A man's chief accessory is his watch. Nowadays, you can get excellent precision from even the cheapest quartz watch, but a mechanical one is still considered much more stylish.

205

Make sure that any metal elements in your jewelry and accessories match each other. A stainless steel, white gold, or platinum watch should be worn with a silver belt buckle, while yellow gold goes better with brass fastenings.

206

207

It is worth investing in a good-quality belt as this can be worn both at home and for work. Before making a very expensive purchase, however, you should mentally run through your collection of shoes. Your money would be wasted if you found you had nothing to wear your new belt with.

Correct belt length is very important. Ideally, the buckle pin should fit through the middle hole (i.e. the third hole of a five-hole belt) with about four inches of leather extending the other side of the buckle.

208

209

If you want to make yourself look slimmer, wear a belt that is slightly too long, never one that is too short. If you have to use the last hole to fasten your belt and only a tiny bit of leather pokes out of the other side of the buckle, it will draw attention to your brimming girth.

210

The color of the belt should match your shoes. This is easy enough if they are both black. Brown is a little more difficult as you have to find the exact shade, in other words, light brown with light brown, chocolate brown with chocolate brown, etc.

211

If you want to be really precise, your wristwatch should also match your belt and shoes. Light-brown leather round your wrist, for example, would clash sharply with black shoes.

212

Colored belts, for example light-blue leather snakeskin effect ones, are best worn with good-quality sports shoes of a similar shade.

213

Not only are sunglasses a practical means of protecting your eyes from UV rays and glare, they are also an important accessory, so choose timeless classics like Ray Ban, or a smart trendy pair.

214

In summer, if you find yourself constantly moving back and forth from bright sunlight to dark interiors, perhaps when you are out shopping, for example, just push your sunglasses up on top of your head in a casual manner.

215

Eyeglasses are all too frequently overlooked, yet, like your haircut, they can make a definitive difference to your appearance. Keep an eye on fashion trends and make sure that your eyeglasses do not become outdated.

If you begin to feel that your colleagues are paying more attention to your eyeglasses than to your personality or professional work, then you may well have chosen a pair that is too conspicuous.

216

217

If you would rather not alter your appearance by wearing eyeglasses, try contact lenses. These have the added advantage of enabling you to follow the latest fashion in sunglasses.

218 Glasses of all description should be kept scrupulously clean. For one thing, you can see through them better and, for another, dirty, speckled lenses give you a slovenly appearance.

219 If you must have your reading glasses hanging round your neck, then at least make sure you have them on a tasteful chain or cord. Gold chains are not really suitable for this purpose.

220

Do not wear sunglasses if the weather is overcast or you are indoors. You would not, after all, feel it necessary to use a parasol in such conditions.

221

If you are restricted to just one wristwatch, then choose a stainless steel one with a metal strap. It will go with any outfit and is suitable for most occasions.

222

The briefcase is often overlooked in terms of the overall budget. Try to avoid making this mistake as a well-made leather briefcase is just as essential to a business outfit as a proper suit.

223

The best types of cuff links are double ones, each consisting of two identical ornamental parts joined by a chain or shank. You can sometimes find particularly fine sets of cuff links in stores specializing in antique jewelry.

224

The best alternative to metal cuff links is braided silk knots. These are available in a wide range of colors and patterns. You sometimes find them displayed for sale in little bonbon dishes next to the cash register in mens' outfitters or shirt-makers.

Never wear suspenders as well as a belt. You must make your mind up in favor of one or the other.

225

226

English-style trousers should be worn with the classic type of suspenders which button onto the inside of the waistband.

227

It is quite acceptable to wear brightly colored suspenders in shades of red, pink, yellow, or light blue with a dark business suit. Even suspenders with motifs on them are permissible, provided you do not choose anything offensive.

228

Every household should have a good umbrella the length of a walking stick. Traditionalists will opt for a black one to take with them to the office. Any dark color with a discreet pattern is equally suitable for both home and office use.

229

Many men apparently believe that a wallet is not at its best until it has been patched up with sticking plaster. Unfortunately, this is not the case, so invest in a good-quality new one.

Put your wallet in the inside breast pocket of your jacket. In this way, you will avoid unsightly bulges in your rear trouser pocket.

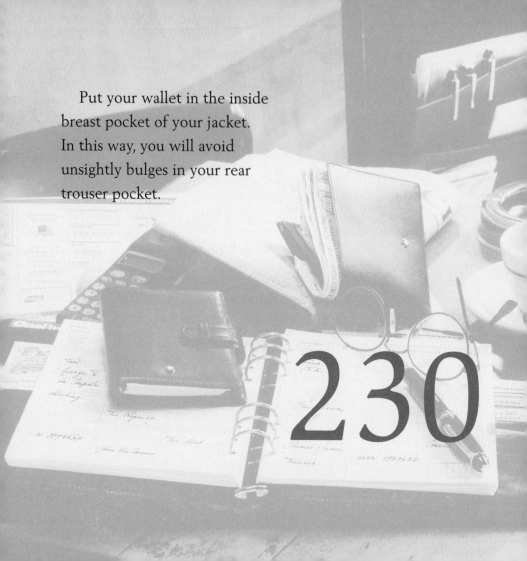

230

Not everyone needs gloves. If you are only carrying your briefcase from the house to the car and then from the office parking lot to your office, you do not require an expensive pair of leather gloves. If you travel by train or bus, however, gloves are essential, if only to protect your hands from dirty handrails and grab straps.

231

232

The color of your gloves is determined by your shoes. Brown gloves to go with brown shoes, black gloves with black ones.

233

On account of their military origins, gray deerskin gloves (as worn by officers) can be worn with black shoes.

234

Your business outfit merits a good quality scarf. Mother's hand-knitted version is better reserved for leisure wear.

235

The appropriate scarf for a well-dressed man should be made from wool, cashmere, silk, or some other natural fiber. Synthetic material should be avoided, not only as a matter of principle (valuable mineral oil is used in its production) but also because it is uncomfortable to wear.

236

If you like the feel of cashmere and the elegant sheen of silk, you can combine the two with a silk scarf lined with cashmere on the inside.

If you decide to splash out on an expensive scarf, you should choose a style that is both timeless and versatile. Reliable classics include dark blue, black, burgundy, or a discreet paisley or polka dots.

237

238

For a really elegant look, wind a fashionable scarf loosely around your neck. Winding it loosely will also keep you warmer (as more air will be trapped inside the scarf as a result).

If you set store on a well-groomed appearance, extend the same courtesy to your luggage. A cheap travel bag looks twice as shabby in the hands of a well-dressed man.

239

STYLISH GROOMING:
HAIR, BEARD, AND BODY

What is it that makes a car desirable? Is it its motor or the chassis? A silly question since a chassis without a motor is just as useless as a motor without a chassis. The same principle applies to hair and body care. Nice hair on its own is not enough to make you elegant, nor will a perfectly tailored suit create the desired effect if the necessary personal hygiene is lacking. Perfection should begin in the bathroom.

240

Beards are viewed differently from one country to another, and from one profession to another. Probably the safest option is to be clean-shaven. Unless, of course, you are meeting up with old friends from your hippy days.

241

In many places, especially in conservative circles, so-called "designer stubble" is regarded simply as a lack of grooming and not as the latest word in fashion. You may be lucky enough not to need to worry about any such disapproval. If not, you had better make regular use of your razor.

242

The very minimum requirement in matters of grooming is a regular haircut. Unfortunately, only very few people are conscientious in this respect.

243

The most important thing in a hairdo is that it should look natural. If it takes you half an hour each morning to make your hair look OK, then there is something amiss.

244

If you are suffering from severe hair loss, it is better to be bold about it than worry about it! It is a sign of self-confidence not to try to conceal thinning hair or bald patches.

245

Your haircut and beard are crucial to your overall appearance. Creating a new look is not just a matter of new clothes, it also means a new hairstyle.

246

If you are in the habit of wearing the same favorite fragrance, then it is more than likely that you apply far too much of it. You become so accustomed to it that you can no longer smell it on yourself. So always remember that less is more.

247

The Americans have coined the perfect phrase for the problem of late-afternoon beard growth, namely the "five o'clock shadow." This is more of a problem for dark-haired men, so if you have a late meeting, or plan to have dinner with someone special, keep a cordless razor in your desk drawer.

248

There is no earthly reason to subject yourself to the torture of splashing on stinging after-shave. It is much pleasanter to use a gentle balsam. You can add fragrance later in the form of eau de toilette.

In the USA, manicured nails are an essential part of a well-groomed appearance. In Europe, however, men with buffed nails might well be viewed with some surprise. Be that as it may, manicured nails do at least look well cared for.

249

250

Hair care should also include those stray hairs in your ears and nose, which can be kept in check with the help of nail scissors or special clippers.

251

Eyebrows with hair sprouting in all directions look very unkempt. Individual hairs do not necessarily have to be plucked into shape, but can be trimmed with scissors by a hairdresser.

252

Dyed or colored hair looks less than natural if it is in stark contrast to the apparent age of the skin. Gray, or even white stubble is also a dead giveaway that you have tampered with your natural hair color.

253

Long hair or a long beard is only acceptable if it is extremely well cared for.

254

As a general principle, any style of beard is acceptable as long as it is not so frivolous that it acts as a magnet for everyone's attention, such as a walrus-style moustache with ends reaching down to your shoulders, or a pointed beard with a twirled end.

255

There are various causes of dandruff and it is often a difficult problem to deal with. If you suffer from this skin condition, you should reinforce any cosmetic measures by choosing the right kind of clothes. Flakes of skin are less conspicuous on light-colored or patterned materials than on self-colored, dark clothes.

Only comb your hair in the bathroom, or when you are alone. The people around you will appreciate it.

256

257

After combing your hair, check your collar and the back of your jacket in the mirror. Long, light-colored hairs look extremely unappetizing on a dark suit and it is too much to expect your partner to be constantly removing stray hairs from your clothes.

258

Have a good look in the mirror after shaving. Small cuts on the neck are easily overlooked, but bright red flecks of blood stand out a mile on a white collar.

259

If you only visit the hairdresser's once every two months, trim your sideburns every four weeks using a good pair of scissors.

260

People's views on gelled or pomaded hair vary considerably. Most people regard hair covered in hair styling products as too oily looking.

261

Avoid using hair sprays or fixatives if possible. For one thing, these styling products make your hair stiff and unnatural-looking, and for another, when dry, they flake onto your jacket collar, looking unpleasantly like dandruff.

TIPS FOR BUSINESS TRIPS

Business trips serve to intensify the existing pressures of everyday life. Instead of a wardrobe full of clothes, you have to make do with a suitcase with a limited selection. Instead of your apartment, you have a hotel room, and instead of your familiar office, you are faced with an unfamiliar conference room. All this may well make it difficult to concentrate on the job in hand. You will find it helps to work out a few survival strategies before your trip.

262

Long car journeys will do your suit no good at
all. It is better to wear casual clothes for driving
in and change into your business suit just before
your meeting. If there is no time or opportunity
to do this, at least remove your jacket during
the journey.

Forgo the complimentary champagne on your outgoing flight to a business meeting. For one thing, you need to keep a clear head, and for another, the smell of alcohol on your breath might make an adverse impression on some people.

263

264

If you are only going on a short flight, try to reduce your luggage to such an extent that you can take it on board with you as hand baggage. You would not be the first person to find yourself with one hour to go before an important meeting, still wearing jeans and a polo shirt, waiting in vain by an empty baggage reclaim belt while your suitcase, containing the business outfit, is speeding through the air on the wrong plane.

265

In the interests of reducing weight on a business trip, forget about your pajamas, slippers, hairdryer, and comfortable cardigan. (If nothing else, it will be less for you to carry from the plane to the hotel.)

A light gray glen plaid would be a practical, all-purpose suit for traveling in. Not only is this type of suit appropriate for all sorts of situations, but it is also extremely stain-resistant.

266

Seasoned air travelers avoid drinking coffee, tea, or tomato juice on their way to a meeting. The risk of a stain is simply too great, as you can hit an air pocket without any warning. So, drink only water on the way there and save the potential stain-causing drinks for your return flight.

267

268

No tie, no roast beef! The grill room of London's Dorchester Hotel insists on a strict dress code. If you are a vegetarian, however, this will not concern you.

269

Traveling light means taking with you only the sort of things that you would not be able to buy in an emergency at your destination. Do not, therefore, lug your heavy sweater along, but buy something warm when you get there if the weather turns cold.

A dark-blue tie is the best choice for a business trip as it goes with any shirt and suit.

270

271

If you tend to warm up quickly once you are indoors, but the weather is cold outside, take a thin, light woolen sleeveless pullover with you when you are traveling. It will keep you warm outdoors and will fit into your briefcase if you find it too hot in the conference room.

272

Businessmen in London wear black shoes with a dark suit. Brown shoes are reserved for weekends in the country.

273

Do not take too many heavy toiletries on a business trip. That large bottle of contact lens solution could be replaced by a travel-sized one, shampoo is provided free of charge in the hotel, hair dryers are also provided for guests' use, and you could always buy a small tube of toothpaste instead of carrying that giant-sized one.

274

Classic Italian style permits brown shoes to be teamed with a dark business suit, although, even in Italy, black shoes are preferred for very formal occasions.

275

Never embark on a business trip wearing new shoes. Even if they initially seem very comfortable, they can turn into instruments of torture within a few hours.

276

If you are handy with an iron, pack your freshly washed shirts straight into your suitcase. Simply borrow an iron at the hotel and press your shirt just before you need to wear it.

Do not embark on a long business trip wearing a linen or cotton suit, unless you have time to change before your important appointment.

277

278

If your suit, jacket, or pants get creased during transport, steam will help get them back into shape again. Close the bathroom window and run a hot shower until the room steams up. Leave the creased garments hanging up in the steamy atmosphere for twenty minutes and the creases will have disappeared.

279

A navy blue suit is the most versatile companion on a short trip. You can wear it with a shirt and tie for your meeting, then, in the evening, wear the jacket with a pair of chinos and an open-necked shirt for dinner in the restaurant.

Never roll up your jacket
sleeves, unless you work in the
red light district.

280

281

A shoehorn, a pair of spare laces, and a clothes brush are essential items for your suitcase. A sewing kit is also important although, in the better hotels, you will find one of these in your bathroom or in a drawer of your room.

282

Be careful about wearing striped ties in Great Britain. It might be embarrassing if you happened to be wearing the same colors as a particular club, regiment, or school and you bumped into people who were legitimately entitled to wear them.

283

If traveling by car, be careful at the filling station not to splash your shoes. Suede shoes, in particular, can be irreparably marked or damaged as a result. Take extra care, also, if you are wearing light-colored trousers, as these will likewise be marked by fuel splashes.

284

If you plan to watch any boat-racing on the Thames, never wear a pink tie, or members of the distinguished Leander Club may well take it amiss.

285

If you are planning to take a pair of brown as well as black shoes with you, a two-tone reversible belt (one side brown, the other black) is a practical accessory for your business trip.

If you have an important business meeting at the end of a long day, always carry a spare pair of socks with you. That embarrassing hole in your sock will inevitably make its appearance at the least opportune moment.

286

When packing, roll up ties and socks and tuck them into the necks of your shirts. This will help protect the collars from creasing while they are in the suitcase and at the same time help you will avoid cramming your suitcase too full.

287

288

If your English business host invites you to a cricket match, please do not wear a yellow-and-red striped tie, as these colors are exclusively reserved for members of the Marylebone Cricket Club.

289

Never wear a white shirt or light-colored cotton suit if your business meeting is taking place over dinner in an Italian restaurant. You are bound to get tomato sauce stains, either self-inflicted or caused by someone else.

290

Take an alarm clock with you when you are traveling. Early morning wake-up calls are often forgotten by the reception desk, causing great inconvenience to the guest.

291

If you are attending a sales meeting in the summer and it is so hot that everything you drink turns into perspiration, resort to a good old-fashioned undershirt. It will absorb any moisture and prevent damp stains on your chest and back.

292

Be cautious about using shoe-polishing machines in hotels. They are usually filled with cheap shoe cream and the rotating brushes can damage delicate leather.

293

Before going on a trip, check the shoelaces of any shoes you are taking. Replace any damaged ones at home rather than having to buy inferior ones at your destination.

EASY WHEN YOU KNOW HOW:
SHOPPING WITH STYLE

Men have a reputation for getting very grouchy when it comes to shopping. Yet, whose idea of a Sunday outing is it to visit a car showroom, or to spend hours wandering round a do-it-yourself store? For many men, this dislike of shopping only surfaces when it becomes necessary to buy a new suit. This has to change!

294

If your jacket is taut across your stomach when buttoned up, it is too small around the waist. If you have the same problem with a jacket in the next size up, a gain in weight over the past few months may be at the root of the trouble.

295

Trousers are the right size around the waist if they just stay up comfortably without the aid of a belt. They should not be any tighter or you will experience difficulties during business luncheons and dinners.

296

You can judge the quality of a suit from the interior finish of the pants. The more detailed the finish, the more expensive the suit.

Never buy a suit made from synthetic material. Natural fibers, like pure virgin wool, are much more comfortable to wear and, apart from this, save on fossil fuels.

297

298

Before buying any new clothes, check what you have in your wardrobe and make a list of what you really need. Only a genius or an ascetic (who possesses no more than two outfits) can retain a mental list of their entire wardrobe.

299

A suit that appears to be a really good buy is more than likely lined with synthetic material, which will come into direct contact with your legs. It is better to resist such apparent bargains as they are guaranteed to make you perspire.

300

You should only buy expensive shoes with stitching round the edge at a store where you can try on the desired style in at least two widths.

301

If you are an inveterate impulse buyer, never buy anything without first thinking about it. It is much better to sleep on it.

302

Experienced air travelers know to buy their Hermès ties from airport stores. You will find that this aristocrat of ties is cheaper there and often available in designs no longer found elsewhere.

Never try on trousers after a lavish meal, otherwise the waist will not fit later. Do not go shopping, therefore, until at least two hours have elapsed since your last meal.

303

It is better to buy three pairs of expensive shoes, which will last you ten or more years if properly taken care of, rather than ten pairs that will wear out after only three years.

304

Never go shopping if you are feeling depressed. You might end up buying too much because you are feeling low.

305

306

Nor should you go shopping when you are in high spirits, otherwise you might end up buying too much out of sheer exuberance.

307

Have little metal plates fitted onto the front of the soles of any new shoes you buy, as this will prevent the toes from wearing out too quickly. The disadvantage of these is that you will no longer be able to walk silently across marble floors.

308

If you want to see a salesman's true colors, then just before making a purchase, say "I'll just have a think about it." If he reacts pleasantly, you will feel like returning to his store.

If you are haggling over the price, then take things a step at a time. Discuss the price first, then the method of payment. If the salesman has already dropped his price by 15 percent, he might reduce it by another four percent for cash.

309

310

In high-class stores, do not be content with a mere five- or ten-percent reduction. After all, these stores have a mark-up of 170 percent (or more) on the original price.

311

Never entrust an intricate alteration to a tailor who has not done any previous work of this kind for you. You can be sure that, according to Murphy's Law, you are bound to have an unpleasant surprise (e.g. you will end up, for some inexplicable reason, with trousers that are much too short).

312

If you need to have jacket sleeves shortened, you must be careful to explain to the tailor exactly how you want the sleeve finished off. You could find, after an alteration, that there is a button short.

313

High-class trousers are sold unhemmed, although you will probably find a length of material for finishing off the hem in one of the pockets. Make sure that your tailor uses the material provided or else you will not get a perfect color match.

314

The quality of your suit will be apparent at the end of a long day behind your desk at the office. If the creases do not disappear overnight, the manufacturer has economized on the quality of the material.

315

Anyone can go a little bit crazy in an attractive store, but if you want to avoid expensive mistakes, have a selection of items sent to your home. In this way, you can view them alongside your existing wardrobe and see what you really need.

316

If you are buying clothes off the rack and cannot make up your mind, always go for the garment that fits best and requires a minimum amount of alteration.

317

No matter what advice the salesman gives you, never allow a jacket to be shortened as this will alter the level of the pockets and make the jacket look out of proportion.

318

Even the most exclusive tailor, shirt-maker, or shoemaker is not averse to a little haggling on the matter of price. The best way to get a reduction is by offering advance payment, as people in this branch of business often have to wait a very long time for payment.

319

When you go shopping, do try to take someone with you who can give you competent advice. Sales staff are not necessarily objective and often lack the motivation to help you make the best of yourself.

320

Do not be frightened to complain about genuine defects. The shopkeeper can send faulty goods back to his supplier and will not suffer any loss personally.

321

The white tacking thread in the shoulder seams of expensive jackets is purely for show. It is by no means a sign of special quality or that the garment is handmade. Tacking the side slits together, however, is a very useful exercise as this will prevent any inadvertent creasing when you hang the jacket back on the rack.

322

The buttonholes on a striped shirt should either have a stripe running right through the middle of them or lie plumb center between two stripes.

Although shoe stores may offer a bigger selection of brand names, men's outfitters display shoes in a more exclusive setting. Above all, you get a better idea of how the shoes will look with the suit and shirt.

323

324

Before sending a suit or coat to the dry-cleaner's, wrap the buttons in aluminum foil to prevent any damage.

If you find the pockets of a new suit sewn up, be very careful when opening them up. Whatever you do, do not simply rip them open! Be extremely cautious, even when you are cutting them open with sewing scissors. You do not want to ruin your purchase before you have even worn it.

325

326

If your shirt collar is pinching, this is not always because it is too tight. It may just be too stiff. In order to be sure, try out a softer style of shirt in the same size.

It is fine for a brand new shirt to be a little on the big side, as the material is bound to shrink to some extent when first washed. If it seems a perfect fit when you try it on in the store, the collar may well become too tight or the sleeves too short later on.

327

328

Never buy a shirt without trying it on first. A reputable store will unpack the shirt for you and let you try it on, or there will be sample shirts (immaculately clean) in all sizes in the changing rooms for you to try.

329

Postpone any less pressing purchases until the sales, when you can acquire top quality at a reasonable price. The most expensive stores can generally offer the biggest reductions, relatively speaking, as they also have the highest profit margins.

330

Be careful when buying abroad. In some countries, you only find out about the value-added tax when you come to pay. When moving around Europe, since the introduction of the euro (worth about a dollar) you no longer have to worry so much about mistakes being made in calculating the exchange rate, except in countries like Britain and Denmark.

331

Do not be reluctant to complain! Shirts should not become two sizes too small after the first ten washes, shoe soles should not come apart after a few wears, and seams should hold for longer than three weeks.

332

When buying a tie, always take whatever clothes with you that the tie is meant to match (in other words, the shirt and suit, or shirt and jacket). Or can you hold the color and pattern in your head?

333

Instead of giving clothes as presents, it is better to give money or gift vouchers. It is almost impossible to choose clothes that are exactly right for someone else. Furthermore, no matter how well-intentioned, it is something of an imposition on the other person's personality to try and dictate what clothes they should wear.

334

Look farther afield! If you are not blessed with many shopping opportunities where you live, but you live close to the border, take a trip to the country or state next door. Apart from anything else, it is useful and informative to have a look at what men's outfitters have to offer in towns on the other side of the frontier.

Many US products are cheaper in the USA than in Europe. Blue jeans are a good example of this.

335

336

Before jumping at a bargain in the sales, ask yourself the following question: Do I like the garment so much that I would have bought it at its original price, or am I just tempted because it is so much cheaper?

You can still find very reasonably priced clothing in Italy if you move off the tourist track. You will find the best bargains in the southern part of the country. For example, in Naples even internationally famous brands are sold at very reasonable prices.

337

338

When buying clothes, the following principle applies: the better the quality, the higher the price. The converse of this is not always true since designer clothes often represent too little quality for too much money.

339

Imitations of luxury goods or jewelry are not only in poor taste, but also injurious to the manufacturers of the original. If you must have a Vuitton, Gucci, or Rolex, then at least get the "real thing."

340

With clothing and accessories, there are three types of supplier: the manufacturers, who market the products themselves; secondly, the designers, who get their designs made up elsewhere; and thirdly the retailers, who market the item under their own label. The best price is generally to be had from the manufacturer.

Factory outlets are useful for timeless or classic brand names. Designer clothes from the previous season are not so interesting.

341

If you are constantly struggling to find a suit that fits, perhaps you should consider having a suit made to measure. This would at least save you all the expensive alterations.

342

343

The price of any clothing is determined by three factors: material costs, manufacturing costs, and profit margin. With any items which are costly to produce – for example, hand-sewn suits, shoes, or ties – the first two factors account for the high price. With designer garments, however, you are often paying primarily for the label.

344

Only buy your clothes from outfitters who have their own workshop for alterations. If anything goes wrong, you can always refuse to pay the balance of the purchase price until everything meets with your satisfaction (unless, of course, you have unwisely parted with the full amount in advance).

Try the garment on after every alteration. If you do not realize that your new pair of pants is too short until just before you need to wear it, you have left it too late.

345

346

Never go shopping just before closing time. You can only hope to find what you want if you have left yourself and the salesman sufficient time. It is also worthwhile remembering that the later in the day it is, the less interest the person serving you will have in your appearance.

Ties should be tried on before purchase. This is the only way to be sure that you are happy with the fabric and the width of the tie.

347

348

You should break in new shoes indoors in your carpeted home. As long as there are no scratches on the soles, you still have the opportunity to change them.

Lace-up shoes should not be too tight across the instep. The lacing should still leave a little gap when the shoe is fastened.

349

350

Smart shoppers will keep a piece of material from a pair of trousers that has been shortened so that they can take it with them on their next shopping trip and get a perfect match for the shirt and tie.

351

Most men only have the waist or length of their trousers altered, ignoring the width of the trouser leg. This is a mistake, because trousers that are too wide at the bottom have the effect of shortening the leg and shoe. The width of the trouser leg should ideally be no more than two-thirds of the shoe length.

352

Trouser turn-ups should not be too narrow. Regardless of the vagaries of fashion, the turn-up should be just under two inches on a man around 6 ft tall.

FAMOUS QUOTATIONS ON STYLE

What is the difference between someone famous and people like us? If we make a pronouncement, it is just something we have said, but if a celebrity expresses an opinion, it becomes a quotation. This is only true, of course, if his wise words are recorded for posterity; deservedly so, at least in the case of the following collection of quotations on the subject of fashion and style.

353

You never get a second chance at making a first impression. *(American saying)*

354

True elegance has just one rule: simplicity.
(Luciano Barbera, designer)

355

Fashion is a transient thing, unlike style. *(Coco Chanel, fashion designer)*

International men's fashion has the Germans to thank for the concept of the "dark suit," a concept which sums up the essence of a gentleman. *(Sir Hardy Amies, couturier)*

356

357

Good clothes open all doors.
(Thomas Fuller, director)

358

I would no more entrust the choosing of my clothes to somebody else than I would allow the most eminent architect to decide on the bed I sleep in.

(Cerruti, fashion designer)

359

I like things that last so long that I can wear them all my life.
(Luca Cordero di Montezemolo, manager)

360

I have an aversion to things that are too expensive.
(Sergio Loro Piana, fabric manufacturer and designer)

361

I see fashion as a means
of creating oneself.
*(Ettore Sottsass, architect
and designer)*

The white T-shirt is perhaps the greatest fashion
innovation of the 20th century.

(Oliviero Toscani, photographer)

362

363

I throw a new suit against the wall a couple of times so that it loses some of its stiffness.

(Fred Astaire, dancer and actor)

364

There is nothing better than a
nice, comfortable baseball cap.
(LL COOL J, Hip-hop artist)

365

I believe that clothes should complement a man's personality, not replace it.
(Jesse Jackson, civil rights leader and politician)

Illustrations:

Asprey & Garrard Ltd, England (339), J. Barbour & Sons Ltd., England (119), Bass & Co., England (68), Belvest S.p.A., Italy (30, 38, 126, 140, 148, 191, 255), Bogner Leather, Germany (208), D'Avenza, Italy (197), Eduard Dressler, Germany (1), Edward Green, England (63, 76, 145, 348), Ermenegildo Zegna, Italy (11, 104, 167, 262, 353), Etienne Aigner AG, Germany (222), Henri Lloyd, England (329), Ignations Joseph Shirts, Germany (19), James Lock & Co., England (133), John Comfort Ltd, England (51), JOOP! GmbH, Germany (282), Louis Vuitton, France (269), Montblanc Deutschland GmbH (203, 230), Officine Panerai, Italy (290), Regent, Germany (175, 215), Tod's, Italy (85)